Mind's Duality in Destiny

MASTERMIND OR MONSTERMIND

Choose to be a Master or a Monster

VAISHNAVI HEND

COPYRIGHT

For information address blink2think14@gmail.com.

TITLE: "MASTERMIND OR MONSTERMIND:

THE MIND'S DUALITY IN DESTINY"

Author: Vaishnavi Hend

Publisher: Vaishnavi Hend

Book Formatting: Vaishnavi Hend

Cover Design: Vaishnavi Hend

EMAIL: blink2think14@gmail.com.

English Non-Fiction Book 1st Edition

ISBN: 978-93-340-7660-8

"To the Divine,

whose guiding presence

has shaped my every word."

PREFACE

In my years of self-introspection, I have realized that the mind is both a mastermind and a monster mind, capable of brilliance and chaos in equal measure. This book is a journey towards a paradox of self-introspection, and an exploration of how our destinies are shaped by the interplay between the binary minds. This book will show you the mirror reflecting the universal truth that, within each of us lies the potential for both greatness and madness.

In the following pages, we will explore how this dynamic shapes our lives and our destinies. As we embark on this exploration together, may we find the courage to embrace both the mastermind and the monster mind within us, and through this understanding, unlock the true potential of our destinies.

In this book, you are not just a reader but a fellow traveler. Together, we will uncover the profound truths about the human mind and its capacity for both greatness and madness. Let us begin this journey with open hearts and curious minds, ready to explore the depths of our inner worlds and emerge with greater clarity and purpose.

DISCLAIMER

This book provides general information only. All the content in this book is unique and plagiarism free. The author has made every effort to ensure accuracy, but assumes no responsibility for errors, omissions, or results from using this information. The author is not liable for any decisions or actions taken based on this book, or for any consequential damages. This book is not professional advice; readers should consult appropriate professionals for their specific situations. References to organizations, products, or individuals do not constitute endorsements.

ACKNOWLEDGEMENT

First of all above and beyond, I would like to thank the universe for reminding me who I am and for showing me how to love myself again. Thank you for always being there for me in this creative journey, for guiding me entirely and for showing from where I can start.

Secondly I am beyond grateful for my parent's unconditional love, support & trust and my sister for her never ending push.

The last note on which I will end is one of the deepest thanks to each and every person who engages with this, you truly are what makes all the hard work worth it. Your support helps ignite my passion and keep the creativity flowing.

Dear Readers thank you for receiving my words and feeling them through yours.

Thank you, for wrapping my words around you and letting them echo.

CONTENT

CHAPTER 9

CHAPTER 1

NATURE OF THE MIND

"Minds are your wings.

You can only fly high,

when you open it

and use its function well."

-Vaishnavi

EXPLORING THE DUAL NATURE OF THE MIND

One summer afternoon, sitting in my room looking outside the window, suddenly a little green cocoon grabbed my attention in the corner of the window struggling to come outside to see the world. Slowly, it started to tremble and delicately crack, revealing it's fragile, folded wings. I witnessed the shy emerging cocoon into a beautiful butterfly, spreading wings and a tiny creature ready to take it's first-ever flight in the air.

You must be thinking, this transformation of a humble caterpillar to a delicate beauty is just a simple act of nature, but what I felt was a self-realization. The beautiful incident of transformation turned my mind into a revelation. I realized about the duality, complexity and the nature of our minds.

The flight of a butterfly seems effortless yet risk and uncertainty are involved in it, parallel to the journey we go through in our minds. We have both a mastermind and a monster mind. The logic and foresight are driven by our mastermind which is the architect of our ambitions; whereas our heavy emotions are ruled by the monster mind, capable of leading us off the rails. The internal struggle between the two minds is similar to the delicate balance of the butterflies during the flight. That's how the butterfly's transformation and balance, set the stage for my exploration towards the mind's duality.

EMBRACING THE BINARY NATURE OF THE MIND

"Mind's depth lies between the extremes of illusions and reality,

An art of balance where it coexists delicately and we call it mind's duality."

-Vaishnavi

A butterfly spreading its newly formed wings personifies the duality. Being fragile and beautiful at the same time, showing strength and struggle, shows the duality of its existence. Just like a butterfly, we all go through transformations in our lives. Our mind goes through metamorphosis, constantly playing between two opposites- our rational thoughts and our emotional impulses.

I have a few questions for you. Have you ever felt the tug of war in your mind when you have choices and how much you feel confused while making any decision? Have you ever felt any difficulty in choosing between two opposing forces? Take a few minutes and answer it.

The human mind always fights a battle between the opposite forces, rationality and emotions, conscious and subconscious, expectations and reality, hopes and desires and the list is long.

Rationality is like a well-designed plan that we make, while dragging towards the adventure is the role of our **Emotions**. Both have their importance, but they don't go together, do they? Think about it: When you're about to make a big decision, like choosing a career or a partner in a relationship, it's like trying to walk on a dangerous rope.

Our minds operate on two levels. The conscious mind controls our thoughts and decision-making. Whereas the subconscious mind hides our memories, habits and acts based on them without us even realizing it.

How often do you feel stuck between fitting into society and being the real you? I am sure it must be a constant inner conflict, like trying to wear two different shoes at the same time.

Let me tell you about my own little story related to this. I was in a high-achieving demanding career, all perfect, but inside, I was dying to write. On one hand, my rational mind was telling me to run towards stability and success, on the other side my emotions were craving for my creative expression. It was like being stuck between ordering a salad and a plate full of chocolate cake in the same meal. Despite my success, I felt a constant inner conflict and the pressure of my professional identity clashing with my emotional need for creative expression.

One evening, I pen down and let my emotions pour out. I experienced a sense of liberation, my emotions were flowing freely on the paper. That was the moment where I found my mind in perfect harmony. That moment was pure magic. It taught me that finding a balance between these aspects of our mind is crucial and it brings you close to clarity. We don't need to choose one over the other but understand that we need both to live our life full of experiences.

By balancing, embracing and acknowledging both sides, we can navigate our life's complexities with more clarity. It’s like adding a pinch of salt to a dessert which is a need to feel the sweetness and correct taste. So next time, remember to listen to both the mastermind and the monster's mind inside you.

THE ORIGIN OF DUALISTIC THINKING

Have you ever thought about the right and wrong theory? Ever thought about why we think in black and white? This habit is in our genes. Our ancestors roamed in jungles and lived their entire lives struggling for survival and food. They had to make quick decisions and for them, the binary thinking (safe or dangerous, good or bad, life or death) was the key to their survival.

Fast forwarding it to the present day, we're still using this old wiring. We categorize people and situations with the same theory. But why does this happen? Our brain is wired to always take shortcuts and snap judgments. It unknowingly tries to simplify things for us, helping us to give a specific direction to make a decision. But I have a question, our ancestors needed it to survive in such a harsh environment but do we need this black and white mentality in this

gray world? Yes, No, Maybe but think about it. Such a dualistic mentality can lead to conflict and misunderstandings, but it can also simplify things for us in a manageable way. By understanding the origin of dualistic thinking, we can explore it beyond its limitations.

Let's embrace the gray areas of this modern world and see what magic happens in the upcoming chapters.

CHAPTER 2

BINARY THINKING

"Tangled thoughts

in the limiting space,

Set them free, to feel the liberation

you've always chased."

-Vaishnavi

Imagine seeing the world from your customized filter that only shows you the extremes of any situation: good or bad, right or wrong. That's **"Binary Thinking"**.

You know what I mean, if you've ever thought in black and white. It makes things simple for us to make quick decisions. But life isn't that simple, right? Then the question arises, how can we escape this mental trap?

COGNITIVE LIBERATION

Let's break this down by the story of Vastavi. She had this weird wiring in her mind of seeing things in contrast. She used to see People, either friends or foes; her Actions were either right or wrong. Her world was limited. Safe but limited.

One day, she met a guy, Vishva who lived in Vastavi's limited areas: **Grey areas**. His life was complex, full of struggles and uncertain experiences that didn't fit into her binary thinking limitations.

When Vishva shared his life's story with Vastavi, she instantly judged him. Further when he explained a choice he made that seemed wrong at first but turned out to be a life-changer for him.

"Wait a minute, so you're saying there's more to it than just right or wrong?" she asked.

"Absolutely," he replied. "Life's all about something more. It's always up to you whether to embrace it or not."

Vishva's words caught her attention. Over the period of time, he encouraged her and she was ready to take her first step towards change. She started by questioning her thought patterns. She started embracing the other side of the world. Slowly, her rigid mindset softened. She began to embrace a growth mindset and practiced empathy.

Vishva recommended books that challenged her viewpoints. She began to embrace that uncertainty is a part of the human experience, its okay not to have all the answers.

Vastavi, finally learned to analyze the situations from multiple angles by asking herself a question that we all should ask ourselves in such situations: "Is there another way to look at this?" It is not easy, but it feels liberating.

She realized that life wasn't just black and white but a beautiful spectrum of colors. This opened new perspectives to her. And you know what? Her world expanded with possibilities she'd never seen before.

Getting free from binary thinking isn't about losing clarity, but about gaining a deeper understanding, and adding more tools to your mental toolkit.

So next time when you find yourself in such a scenario of an all-or-nothing mindset, take a step back. Ask questions, embrace the gray areas, and see what new possibilities emerge out of it.

CHAPTER 3

THE ILLUSION OF DUALITY

"Illusion reigns, where the choices raise

Mind diverges,

without leaving any trace.

Yet answers resides,

somewhere within the mess,

Find them in the duality's embrace."

-Vaishnavi

MAKING DECISIONS BEYOND DUALITY

Ever feel stuck between two choices either this or that? That's the real trap for you when it comes to "**Making Decisions".** This is the illusion of dualistic thinking. But, why is this dual mindset so limiting and how can you escape the illusion of choice? Let's break it down.

Dualistic thinking forces you to see the world from the filter of black-and-white only. It simplifies our complex issues, but life isn't that simple. You miss out on the possibilities that lie between the extremes. The possibilities are endless if you look beyond it.

Let's again delve into my own story: Continuing the same story further, I found myself at a crossroad, between staying in a high-paying, soul-sucking job or a low-paying start towards the thing I was passionate about. I was stuck in binary choices. I felt trapped until I found the solution. I found that I could combine my writing skills with my passion for society. I started exploring different ideas and eventually landed here, in front of you, where I can have both a good pay and meaningful work.

Seeking diverse viewpoints, and opening to multiple possibilities (beyond my obvious choices), I expanded my cognitive mindset. My journey of breaking dualistic thinking revealed a broader spectrum of choices, leading to more satisfying and innovative decision-making.

CHAPTER 4

THE COMPLEXITY AND THE GRAY THOUGHTS

"Countless complexities,

in the realm of gray,

Tangled thoughts,

and I can't find my way.

But within my mind,

where light showers its rays,

Navigating me through, day by day."

-Vaishnavi

We live in a world that has two sides, and every time you're being forced to pick one side because you feel stuck between the two choices. But is it so? Is it that easy to pick one? No, it's not, life has its third side too- "**The Grey Side**".

Let me tell you, life is not that straightforward. It's messy, interconnected, and beautifully complicated. You've to learn to embrace the gray areas and navigate the complexities that comes with them. But, how to understand complexity?

Complexity is all about seeing the bigger picture. Have you ever tried jigs? Well, I did and that's the time when you see or I must say imagine seeing the bigger picture, finding the missing pieces while trying to solve the puzzle. That's what it looks like to tackle these issues without acknowledging their interconnectedness. By doing so, you can avoid the trap of oversimplification and develop a more refined perspective.

Embracing the gray areas means being open to multiple viewpoints. Imagine hosting a party and inviting guests with diverse opinions. Each one brings something valuable and new to the table. I know, not every dish will hit the spot, but it will lead us to know or to try something new, and it will open up to more discussions. It's all about flexible thinking rather than shutting down conversations with a rigid mentality.

To live in the gray area means to get comfortable with uncertainty. You have to make the decision even if you don't have the complete information and you have to be ready to spin the wheel when new data comes in.

At last, embracing complexity is boosting empathy. When you accept the fact that, issues has its own shade card of a variety of colors in it, you become more understanding. It's not like you can't have your principles, it's about cultivating a mindset that values depth, diversity, and adaptability, and you don't need to become an indecisive individual for that. By doing so, you'll be ready to tackle the critical challenges with wisdom and compassion.

CHAPTER 5

MASTER VS. MONSTER

"Master and monster,

within a single mind,

Two unlike faces but likely entwined.

One emerges,

by showering wisdom of light,

While the other fades,

in the darkness of night."

-Vaishnavi

Imagine, you have a dilemma in your mind, where your destructive tendencies of mind are constantly clashing with your rational instincts. That is the real battle between your monster mind and mastermind, like having a devil on one shoulder and an angel on the other, both trying to grab your attention.

THE BATTLE WITHIN:

INNER DEMONS

VS.

INNER MASTERS

Did you ever play a never-ending wrestling match between your doubts and desires?

Let me give you a prime example of this daily struggle; Sam, a young talented artist having a mind full of uncontrolled thoughts. The hero and a demon are both installed in his mind. These demons whisper constant nonsense and negative stuff while the masters whisper sweet encouraging songs, always pushing him toward positivity.

One day he got a major moment to exhibit his art. But as soon as he got the opportunity, his inner demons (negative thoughts) popped out, "Are you talented enough to get this opportunity?", "what if you fail?

He was ready to step back but the masters (positive thoughts) reminded him of his hard work; the immense joy his art brings every time after the completion of his artwork. And by listening to them he decided to take that step forward.

The journey wasn't all smooth. At times, he felt like those demons were winning. But every time, his masters guided him back into the light. Slowly, Sam realized he was way more capable than the demons in his mind.

Sam's story shows us the fact that the toughest battles are fought within. Defeating your inner demons and embracing your masters isn't easy. It's an ongoing process. But as long as you believe in yourself, you'll emerge victorious, just like Sam.

This battle between the monster and the master mind is something we all face. It's not just Sam's story, it's everyone's.

Listening to the master needs real practice and exercise just like we go to the gym for the fitness of our body, but this time we need the gym for our brain. It takes self-awareness, discipline, and a lot of effort.

THE MONSTER MIND UNLEASHED

Let's talk about a story of the darker aspects of our minds. This isn't a horror story, but it sure can feel like one.

It's my story. When I started writing, I got stuck in my creative writing blocks which gave me nightmares. My inner turmoil and blurry vision was reflecting in my writings. But then, I confronted my traumas. By embracing my vulnerability, I reclaimed my control, transforming the darker aspects of my mind by showering light on them.

Confronting our inner darker demon is the first step toward healing and growth. Embrace your vulnerabilities and past pain to find redemption.

THE MASTERMIND EMERGES

Mastermind emerges when you start nurturing the light within, tapping into your inner potential to become a guiding force in your life. The journey of self-discovery, the journey of not being smarter but wiser. It's all about aligning your actions with your values and passions.

Consider my story again- I was a shy writer hesitant to share my work. But, by listening to my inner master, I embraced a self-discovery journey and wrote the reality of my life that was reflecting my dreams.

TRANSFORMING MONSTERS INTO MASTERS

Obstacles are part of any journey, but it takes you toward mastery. These can be self-doubt, fear, competition or change, the obstacles can be internal or external.

The key here is to see these obstacles not as an obstacle but as an opportunity to grow. It's like blending diverse things, skills and perspectives. Just like cooking the best dishes from unexpected combinations of different ingredient.

Another aspect is to embrace diversity. By working with people from different backgrounds and disciplines, you gain fresh insights and approaches.

Obstacles are monsters; but remember, your monsters aren't here to defeat you. They're here to transform you. You just have to embrace them, integrate their lessons, and turn them into your masters.

CHAPTER 6

THE YIN AND YANG OF THE MIND

"Yin and yang, the two opposite forces,
Inside the mind they find their place.
Find the balance in cosmic space,
Where unity meets diversity,
by divine grace."

-Vaishnavi

BALANCING OPPOSING FORCES

You must have heard about Yin and Yang, if not then let me tell you, it's a Chinese philosophy of balancing two opposite energies. Let's relate this philosophy to our minds.

Imagine the two characters: Null, an architect and Neel, a constructor. Null is all Yin—quiet, creative, contemplative, and cool-minded. Whereas Neel is all Yang—active, energetic, and always ready to go.

One day their village faced a crisis, a severe storm destroyed their main bridge. The villagers asked Null and Neel for a solution.

So, what do you think, what did they do? Let me answer this, recognizing their strengths, they decided to combine their forces. Null sketched a thoughtful plan considering the river's flow, and he designed the blueprint of the bridge. Neel gathered materials and people, ready to get to work. Null's thoughtful designs and Neel's energetic execution created a strong, beautiful bridge.

This collaboration taught them the importance of balance. Null realized that without action, his designs would remain just designs. Neel learned that without thoughtful planning, his efforts might be wasted. Together, they found that middle spot between thoughts and action.

We all have Yin and Yang within us. To balance them we just need some time to meditate, relax in a quiet space and connect with our inner selves. But we also need to get out there, set goals, take action, and engage with the world.

Yin and Yang are the parts of your mental toolkit. By nurturing both aspects, you can achieve a balanced state of mind. Trust me by doing this, your mind, life and soul each one of them will thank you.

CHAPTER 7

BEYOND GOOD OR EVIL:

MORALITY

"Morality beyond good and evil,

A mind's beautiful intention to choose

with your free will."

-Vaishnavi

What is Morality?

It's all about good and evil, right and wrong. But, remember we live in a gray world and not in black and white, just forget what your teachers told us when you were a kid.

You see the hero in him and a villain in her, but life isn't a fiction book. Sometimes the heroes and villains switch roles or sometimes they share the same table. But, understand sometimes they both could be right.

Radhi is a leader who lives in a small town. One day, a rich developer humbly requested her permission to cut down a beautiful forest to build a hospital. Now that's the classic example of what I was talking about- good vs. evil, right? What if you face such a moral dilemma just like Radhi, what will you choose? Will you save lives or will you save the forest?

But she chose to pause for a while. She found the middle way by considering all the alternatives like fundraising and finding a compromise with the developer. She offered a barren land to the developer to build a hospital. She navigated her way to a solution where she managed to balance both lives and nature.

To be honest, the Moral of the story is all based on the Morality we hold.

Our upbringing, cultural, norms and mentality shape our moral beliefs. So, next time when you feel stuck on making a moral decision, stop right there, don't just jump to conclusions. Remember, Radhi's story of morality and her middle way of finding a solution.

CHAPTER 8

THREADS OF DESTINY

"You make promises, under the sun,

That your journey will never end

until it's done.

But threads of fate,

has a different plan to run,

Beautifully knitting your destiny,

one by one."

-Vaishnavi

CHOICES

THAT SHAPES OUR FUTURE

Let's talk about choices. You know, every day we have something to think about and we rarely stop it. Ever found yourself doing so?

Another big question here is- Is your choice yours or it's just another page in the book of destiny? Are we humming to our tune or just lip-syncing the already-composed song of our lives?

The essence of choice is all related to humans, it's your superpower. But what about fate then? What if the universe has already designed the blueprint of the path to our destination? Its life's massive jigsaw puzzle and we're just trying to find our piece. In the intersection of choice and fate, what do you choose? Think about it and answer.

At that time, you should admit that sometimes you have no clue what's going on. It's about seeing the connections, and recognizing that even the smallest decision can bring a big change. Each thread of fate represents the choices we make. Every decision you make, no matter how, adds to your destiny. Choices always come with consequences. Life is a living, breathing masterpiece. It's not a straight line but a tangled web of possibilities. You're constantly adding new threads and adjusting the old ones.

Let me tell you, the path you choose is a reflection of your deepest self. It's the blend of your hopes, fears, and dreams, all tangled up with the threads of destiny.

"Our destinies are co-created by a beautiful, chaotic mix of free will and cosmic forces."

We're not puppets here, we have the power to choose and shape our destiny, and we have our free will. We have the power to drive our car on the path of life to reach our destinies. Always remember, we are the driving masters of our destiny, not just a passenger.

So, whenever you find yourself standing at the crossroads of choice, try not to find clear solutions but rather the art of synthesis. I am suggesting you to blend the duality, just like finding harmony in the chaos.

Guided by our gut feeling, trusting our instincts, when we step boldly into the unknown, we find our truest selves.

CHAPTER 9

SHAPING THE DESTINY

"The choices we make,

to take the high flight,

Without navigating dualities,

we want to shape our destiny, right? "

-Vaishnavi

NAVIGATING DUALITIES TO SET UP ONE'S DESTINY

Navigating duality is like trying to drive a car in heavy rains while following a Google map directing you in some foreign language you don't know. It's not just a journey from here to somewhere. It's an adventure through our consciousness.

You have to actively engage with these dualities to set up one's destiny. By sitting back, you can't just hope for the best. It's about choosing to pick yourself up after every failure and celebrate every victory, no matter what.

The mirror not only reflects your face but it also reflects your shadow soul, just like that, this is the journey of dealing with your shadow side, **"The Journey of Self- Introspection."**

By confronting your fears, and embracing your limitations, you can navigate the complexities of your mind. You have to see both the light and the shadow within you and understand that they both have a role to play.

The real magic happens when you start seeing obstacles as your friend, not an enemy. Night doesn't exist without day; light doesn't exist without dark. Understanding this on a deeper level will lead you to realize who you are and what you're here to do.

EMBRACING THE JOURNEY

Let's do an activity, try to imagine what you're going to read now:

You are standing on the top of the mountain looking at the setting sun, leaving behind the colorful shades in the sky and thinking about your life's journey filled with battles you fought and lessons you learned. The open sky in front of you is vast and unknown with endless possibilities, but you're not afraid to fly high, you're all ready to embrace whatever comes your way.

You've all the wisdom of experience just because you know yourself. You've learned to navigate and face all the dualities, and despite doubt, you've discovered yourself.

You know that the greatest journey is the one that leads back to yourself. Every choice you made, every path you took, has led you here on the top. You realize that a journey isn’t about reaching a final destination but about embracing every twist and turn along the way.

The stars begin to twinkle, you smile, feeling a sense of peace, and the gentle breeze on your face. At that moment, understanding that your destiny wasn't navigating you to find a specific place but it was navigating you to discover yourself. It was showing you the direction to balance the light and shadow within you.

With clarity of mind, you are ready to step forward and face the unlimited possibilities of the future; because you know, you are limitless. As the sun sets below the horizon, you open your arms, embracing reality, knowing that no matter where the winds of fate may blow, you are the creator of your destiny.

Now come to reality, and understand, time is calling you to take an action and to make a decision, reminding you that within the chaos of your mind lies the strength to navigate through dualities. You have to deal with monsters in your mind by listening to the masters.

Hold the pen with a tight grip and write your own story. Navigate this journey with courage, wisdom, trust, a little charm and zero worry.

"Dear Readers,

Thank you for receiving my words

and feeling them through yours."

An Ardent Author, skilled in the art of weaving emotions and perspectives into captivating prose and poetry. She believes in the transformative power of words, channeling compressed voices, thoughts, emotions, and desires into her literary creations. Her writing vibrates with the universal tones of what makes us human oscillating and appeals to readers as much for curious explorations of emotionality. Her work resonates with readers, inviting them to explore the depths of human experience through her unique vibrations.

VAISHNAVI HEND

Instagram Handle- blink2think

Email- blink2think14gmail.com

www.ingramcontent.com/pod-product-compliance
Lightning Source LLC
Chambersburg PA
CBHW062113160726
48282CB00026B/786
* 9 7 8 9 3 3 4 0 7 6 6 0 8 *